Epilogue

_____

To create you need to imaginate. Thats how all of the most amazing structures and places were made. You always have to imagine before you create. Take me for example- For me to make my Proffeser Awesomeness YouTube channel I had to think about what type of content that I was going to put up there. So as you see to create you always need to imaginate.

Create

_____

Creation…. is incredible in so many ways. From building the worlds tallest building to making the most powerful microchip ever- we will never stop creating. I follow three steps to help me create: Imaginate-Plan-Build. You wouldn't have a house or even be reading this page or word if it weren't for those people that made creating possible. You can build the worlds tallest building or another Millennium Force and have it voted the best roller coaster in the world for 10 years straight, but in order for all of that to happen you need to imagine and plan and then create. Take Steve Jobs and Steve Wozniak, they had a dream to create a computer smaller than the computers then. So they created the Apple I.

It never really succeeded so they went back and made the Apple II. It started to boom. And they kept going back and forth making new things until they unveiled one of the worlds best known computers-the Macintosh (or Mac). See what I'm getting at? They never stopped doing what they loved and they made something incredible.

That's Creation.

Imaginate

Imagination is so crazy and awesome and incredible. Thats what helped us create some of the craziest things. It helped us build the Burj Khalifa, the worlds tallest building. It helped us build our houses, our neighborhoods, and our towns and cities, it helped us create who we are. Imagination is where you think of something and then make it happen. It motivates you. Like it helped me make this book. This world wouldn't be the place we know now with cities and stores and people. It would be just a plain desert with just people on it. Take John J. Raskbob for another example.

He wanted to build the worlds tallest building in the middle of New York City. He wanted to win the race for the sky against the Chrysler Building, and he sure did. He imagined and dreamed to make a giant building, and that motivated him to make the Empire State Building. Now its one of the most visited places in the world. He used his imagination to motivate him to make that wonderful, glorious building we know today. So no matter what we dream of, just know that you can do it- you just have to be dedicated enough to do it and you most importantly-

Have to imaginate.

Use It

_____

U can create amazing things like Disney World or Disneyland if you just Create and Imaginate. In order for that to happen you need to learn how to Create and Imaginate. So what I like to do is Imaginate what I want to make. Then I pick up a piece of paper and draw what I have Imagined. I then get supplies and make the thing I imagined and drew. It will take time to do but in the end you have made your very own masterpiece. Do you see what I mean? Using Create-Imaginate can help you do so many things.

Keep Going

_____

You need motivation to do things. We all need motivation to do things. Like Walt Disney said " The only way to get started is to quit talking and begin doing" and " All our dreams can come true, if we have the courage to pursue them". To be motivated to do something you have to have courage. You have to be able to push yourself to do something, and if you do that you can build Disney World.

Encouraging Sayings

" The only way to get started is to quit talking and begin doing"- Walt Disney

"Whatever you are be a good one"- Abraham Lincoln

"Because the people who are crazy enough to thing they can change the world are the ones that do"- Steve Jobs

"Your only given one spark of madness, You mustn't use it"- Robin Williams

"Don't chase people. Be yourself, do your own thing and work hard"- Will Sm th

So as you see its not that easy to create and imaginate.

But we have always managed to do it because we humans are all one team and we work together to pull it off.

Do you see what im getting at? In order to do all things you always need someone to help you either do it by yourself or to help you build a huge thing.

But to do that we all have to love each other and get to know each other.

Then you all get together and Create-Imaginate.

After that you build, draw, imaginate, finish, and after all of that what do you have? A masterpiece.

And after that masterpiece has been made you can then see what you have made. Good or bad just know that its your very own master piece that you made up and built.

And the way you did it is by motivation, and most importantly creation or imagination or you can just say-

Create-Imaginate

www.ingramcontent.com/pod-product-compliance
Lightning Source LLC
Chambersburg PA
CBHW041830280526
45792CB00006B/2044